CELEBRATIONS

By Joanna Brundle

KidHaven
PUBLISHING

A Look at Life Around the World

Published in 2019 by
KidHaven Publishing, an Imprint of Greenhaven Publishing, LLC
353 3rd Avenue
Suite 255
New York, NY 10010

Designer: Jasmine Pointer
Editor: Kirsty Holmes

Photocredits: Abbreviations: l-left, r-right, b-bottom, t-top, c-center, m-middle. All images are courtesy of Shutterstock.com. With thanks to Getty Images, Thinkstock Photo and iStockphoto. Front cover – beeboys, AJP, Saigoneer. 2 - Quetzalcoatl1. 4t - Monkey Business Images. 4b - Taras Vyshnya. 5 – IVASHstudio. 6 – szefei. 7 - topten22photo. 8 - Kristina Sophie. 9l – espies. 9r – adycreative. 9b – Rimma Bondarenko. 10t - CP DC Press. 10b - Calin Stan. 11 – StanislavBeloglazov. 12m - Dina Julayeva. 12r – BonnieBC. 13l – AGCuesta. 13r - David Litman. 14 - S.Borisov. 15 - marilyn barbone. 16 – SMDSS. 17t – reddees. 17b – Peter Gueth. 18 - Noam Armonn. 19 – arapix. 20t - Joseph Sohm. 20b - Milleflore Images. 21t - Stuart Monk. 21b – Migel. 22l - topten22photo. 22r Guitar Studio.

All facts, statistics, web addresses and URLs in this book were verified as valid and accurate at time of writing. No responsibility for any changes to external websites or references can be accepted by either the author or publisher.

Cataloging-in-Publication Data

Names: Brundle, Joanna.
Title: Celebrations / Joanna Brundle.
Description: New York : KidHaven Publishing, 2019. | Series: A look at life around the world | Includes glossary and index.
Identifiers: ISBN 9781534528437 (pbk.) | ISBN 9781534528451 (library bound) | ISBN 9781534528444 (6 pack) | ISBN 9781534528468 (ebook)
Subjects: LCSH: Festivals--Juvenile literature. | Holidays--Juvenile literature. | Rites and ceremonies--Juvenile literature.
Classification: LCC GT3933.B78 2019 | DDC 394.26--dc23

Printed in the United States of America

CPSIA compliance information: Batch #BW19KL: For further information contact Greenhaven Publishing LLC, New York, New York at 1-844-317-7404.

Please visit our website, www.greenhavenpublishing.com. For a free color catalog of all our high-quality books, call toll free 1-844-317-7404 or fax 1-844-317-7405.

CONTENTS

Words that look like this can be found in the glossary on page 23.

WHAT ARE CELEBRATIONS?

Celebrations are times when people come together to mark special events. In this book, we will be traveling around the world, looking at how people celebrate. As you read, think about celebrations that you have taken part in. What made them special?

Celebrations mark important stages in our lives, like the birth of a new baby.

New Year is often celebrated with fireworks, like this spectacular display in Sydney, Australia.

This Hindu family is celebrating a wedding.

Special <u>customs</u>, food, music, and clothing can all be part of celebrations. Celebrations can be part of a person's religion or they may be a part of family life. People use celebrations to give thanks and to show what is important to them and their <u>culture</u>.

CHINESE NEW YEAR

Chinese New Year is celebrated by Chinese people all around the world. It is a time for new beginnings and for celebrating the coming of spring. People wear red clothes and children receive gifts of money in red envelopes, called hongbao.

Gifts of tangerines and oranges <u>symbolize</u> wealth.

Fireworks are an important part of the celebrations. Legend says that they scare away a beast called Nian who tries to attack villagers.

People hold a <u>banquet</u> for family and friends. Festive parades take place with dancers, acrobats, and drums. People dress up as dragons or lions and perform a special dance as part of the parades.

HOLI

Holi is an <u>ancient</u> Hindu festival that can last up to seven days. It is also known as the Festival of Colors. It celebrates the beginning of spring and the victory of goodness, peace, and love over evil. People celebrate by lighting bonfires and throwing water and colored powders called gulal at one another.

In the evenings, people visit family and friends and carry on celebrating. Many special foods are eaten. These include:

Gujiyas – sweet dumplings filled with nuts, dates, or coconut.

Malpuas – pancakes fried and dipped in sugar.

Thandai – a special drink made with rose petals, almonds, and milk.

CARNIVALS

Before Easter, Christians sometimes give up certain foods during a time called Lent. They use this time to think about the importance of God's teachings in their lives. Carnivals with colorful, noisy parades are often held just before Lent starts.

At the Venice Carnival in Italy, people wear beautifully decorated masks and headpieces.

Over five days, up to ten million people go to see the Rio de Janeiro carnival and street parties in Brazil.

The carnival celebrated in Rio de Janeiro dates back to 1723 and is the biggest and most famous carnival in the world. The most spectacular part is the Samba Parade. <u>Samba schools</u> spend months preparing breathtaking costumes and <u>floats</u> for the parade.

11

DÍA DE LOS MUERTOS

People dress up and wear skull masks or makeup.

Marigolds

Día de los Muertos takes place every year in Mexico and other countries, including Spain and Brazil. The name means "Day of the Dead." This isn't a sad festival, though. In fact, it is a joyful celebration of the lives of people who have died.

During the celebrations, people remember their loved ones. Children are remembered on the 1st of November and adults are remembered on the 2nd of November. People set up small altars called ofrendas at home. The ofrendas are decorated with photographs, candles, marigolds, and sugar skulls called calaveras.

This ofrenda has also been decorated with a sweet bread called pan de muerto.

Shops and markets sell brightly colored skull masks.

CHRISTMAS

Christmas markets selling decorations, gifts, and food are popular in Germany.

Christmas is celebrated lots of different ways in different places. In Norway, Denmark, and Sweden, for example, presents are given and a Christmas meal is eaten on the 24th of December. In the United Kingdom, these things happen on the 25th of December.

Many different foods are eaten around the world to celebrate Christmas. In China, people exchange apples wrapped in colored paper on Christmas Eve. In Denmark, a rice pudding made with almonds is eaten. A whole almond is hidden in the rice pudding, and whoever finds it gets a special gift.

In Italy, a type of bread called panettone is often baked as a gift for friends and family.

OTHER RELIGIOUS CELEBRATIONS

Diwali is a five-day celebration, also known as the Festival of Lights. It is celebrated by Hindus all over the world, especially in India, Malaysia, Nepal, and Sri Lanka. People light small oil lamps called diyas to invite Lakshmi, the goddess of good fortune, into their homes.

People use colored rice powder to make rangoli patterns.

Followers of the Sikh religion in India, Canada, the United States, and the United Kingdom celebrate the birthday of Guru Nanak. Guru Nanak was the person who began the Sikh religion.

During the celebration, people sing, dance, pray, and light candles.

Vesak is celebrated by Buddhists in countries such as China and Thailand. During Vesak, people celebrate the life and teachings of Buddha, the founder of Buddhism.

Vesak Celebrations, Indonesia

Hanukkah lasts eight days and is celebrated by Jewish people. A special candlestick with nine branches, called a menorah, is used to celebrate Hanukkah. Another candle is lit each evening. You light the candles with a different candle, called the shamash.

Hanukkah celebrates a <u>miracle</u> that happened long ago when a lamp that only had enough oil for one day managed to stay alight for eight days.

Eid al-Fitr is celebrated by Muslims all around the world. It is a joyful celebration at the end of the holy month of Ramadan. Special prayers are said and Muslims celebrate with family and friends. People wear new clothes, eat sweet foods, and give one another gifts.

During Ramadan, Muslims do not eat during daylight hours.

Traditional foods for Eid al-Fitr celebrations include these Eid cookies.

NATIONAL CELEBRATIONS

In the United States, the 4th of July is Independence Day. On this day in 1776, the United States became <u>independent</u> from Great Britain. People celebrate with parades, fireworks, and barbecues.

Australia Day is on the 26th of January and celebrates Australian history and culture.

Some countries have national days named after <u>saints</u>. The people of Ireland celebrate St. Patrick's Day on the 17th of March. The day has become a celebration of Ireland in countries all around the world.

St. Patrick's Day parade, with traditional Irish costumes, in New York

People in France celebrate their national day, known as Bastille Day, on the 14th of July.

Bastille Day parade, Paris, France

SONGKRAN

Songkran celebrates the New Year in Thailand, Laos, Myanmar, and Cambodia. People clean their houses to bring them good fortune. They spend time with their families and show <u>respect</u> for older relatives by pouring water over their hands. Everyone has fun soaking one another with water guns.

People honor Buddha by sprinkling perfumed water over statues of him.

GLOSSARY

ancient	belonging to the very distant past and no longer in existence
banquet	a large, grand dinner
culture	the ideas and way of life of a group of people
customs	traditional ways of behaving or doing things
floats	spectacular displays mounted on a platform and pulled along as part of a parade
independent	separate from
miracle	an extraordinary event thought to show God's power
respect	caring for the rights, wishes, and feelings of others
saints	especially good, holy people believed to be in heaven
samba schools	dance clubs or schools that teach the samba, a lively rhythmic dance
symbolize	to be something you can see that stands for something you cannot see, like good luck

INDEX